Spanish Tapas

TRADITION

50 Easy-to-Follow Tapas Recipes Celebrating the Richness of Spanish Gastronomy

James Stott

Dear fellow food enthusiasts, we trust you're about to embark on a flavorful journey through the world of Spanish Tapas. As you savor each recipe and explore the rich tapestry of flavors, we'd be delighted if you could share your thoughts on Amazon with a review, via the QR code link here.

To be notified of all new books and ensure that you never miss a free book download opportunity then please send an email with your name to any of the following to note your interest and get the links to new releases and all free books. We will not share or spam your email address

For personal development books, email Development@SoReadyToRead.com
For cookbooks, email Cookbooks@SoReadyToRead.com
For crime books, email Crime@SoReadyToRead.com
For technology, blockchain, and their uses books, email Technology@SoReadyToRead.com
To receive notifications for all book genres, send an email with your name to All@soreadytoread.com
Please feel free to share these addresses

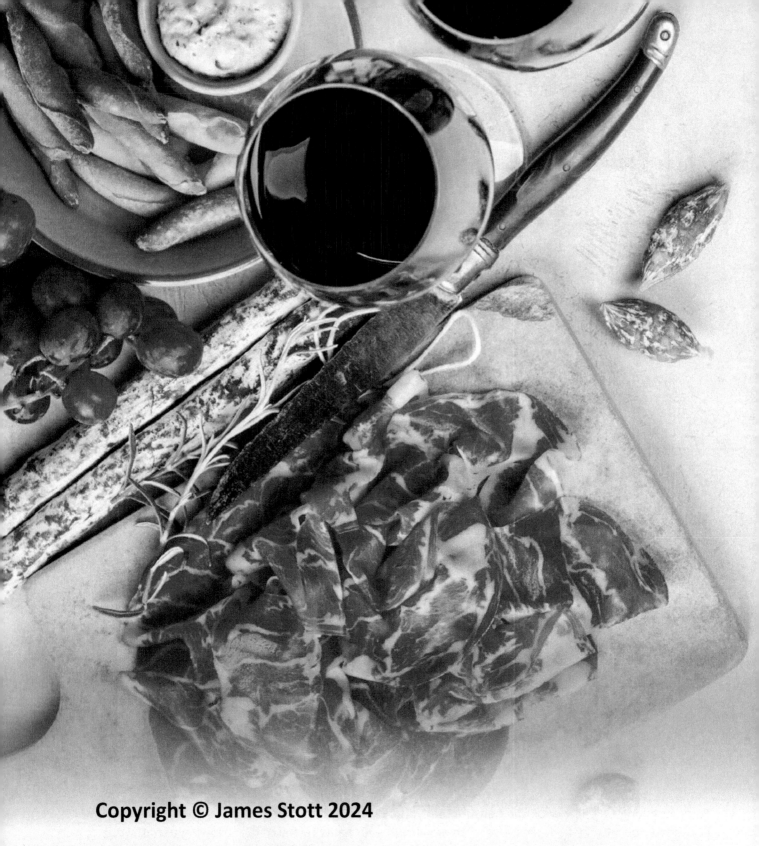

Copyright © James Stott 2024

Introduction

Welcome to "Tapas Tradition," your gateway to mastering the art of Spanish tapas. This collection is more than just a cookbook—it's a passport to experiencing the warmth and conviviality of Spanish culture, one bite-sized delight at a time.

In the following pages, we celebrate the rich tapestry of flavors that define Spain's favorite culinary pastime. Tapas are not just appetizers; they are a way of life. From bustling bars in Madrid to seaside bistros in Catalonia, tapas are the heartbeat of social gatherings. This cookbook invites you to bring that pulsating energy into your home with 50 recipes that span the spectrum from traditional to modern, simple to sophisticated.

With "Tapas Tradition," we aim to simplify the art of tapas for chefs of all skill levels. You'll learn how to create everything from savory Albóndigas (meatballs) to sweet and crunchy Churros. We include the classics like Patatas Bravas and Pimientos de Padrón, alongside contemporary twists that still respect the essence of Spanish cooking.

Each recipe is a celebration, designed to be shared and savored. They encourage you to linger over the dining table, fostering conversations and creating memories. As you delve into this book, you'll discover not just the flavors of Spanish cuisine but the very soul of Spain's eating culture.

Prepare your kitchen for a fiesta of flavors as you embark on this gastronomic journey. Whether you're throwing a tapas party or simply spicing up your meal repertoire, "Tapas Tradition" will be your companion, guiding you through the succulent world of Spanish gastronomy. It's time to eat, enjoy, and explore—buen provecho!

Contents

Nutrition

Calories: 250, Protein: 3g,
Carbohydrates: 40g, Fat: 10g

Prep Time:
15 Mins

Cook Time:
25 Mins

Serving: 4

INGREDIENTS

- 4 large potatoes, peeled and cut into cubes
- Vegetable oil for frying
- Salt to taste
- For the spicy tomato sauce:
- 2 tablespoons olive oil
- 2 cloves garlic, minced
- 1/2 teaspoon smoked paprika
- 1/4 teaspoon cayenne pepper
- 1 can (15 oz) crushed tomatoes
- Salt to taste

PATATAS BRAVAS

INSTRUCTIONS

1. Heat vegetable oil in a deep fryer or large deep skillet over medium-high heat.
2. Once the oil is hot, add the potato cubes and fry until golden and crispy, about 10-15 minutes. Remove the potatoes with a slotted spoon and drain on paper towels. Sprinkle with salt.
3. For the spicy tomato sauce, heat olive oil in a saucepan over medium heat. Add garlic, smoked paprika, and cayenne pepper, and sauté for 1-2 minutes until fragrant.
4. Stir in the crushed tomatoes and bring to a simmer. Reduce heat and simmer for about 10-15 minutes until the sauce thickens. Season with salt to taste.
5. Serve the fried potatoes with the spicy tomato sauce on top or on the side.

Nutrition

Calories: 210, Protein: 24g,
Carbohydrates: 2g, Fat: 12g

**Prep Time:
10 Mins**

**Cook Time:
10 Mins**

Serving: 4

INGREDIENTS

- 1 lb. large shrimp, peeled and deveined
- 3 tablespoons olive oil
- 6 cloves garlic, thinly sliced
- $\frac{1}{4}$ teaspoon red chili flakes (optional)
- Salt and freshly ground black pepper to taste
- Fresh parsley, chopped for garnish
- Lemon wedges for serving

GAMBAS AL AJILLO (GARLIC SHRIMP)

INSTRUCTIONS

1. In a large skillet, heat olive oil over medium heat.
2. Add the garlic and red chili flakes (if using), and sauté for about 1-2 minutes until the garlic is golden.
3. Add the shrimp to the skillet, season with salt and black pepper, and cook for about 2-3 minutes on each side or until the shrimp are pink and opaque.
4. Remove from heat, garnish with fresh parsley, and serve hot with lemon wedges on the side.

Nutrition

Calories: 250, Protein: 12g,
Carbohydrates: 30g, Fat: 10g

Prep Time:
15 Mins

Cook Time:
30 Mins

Serving: 4

INGREDIENTS

- 4 large potatoes, thinly sliced
- 1 onion, thinly sliced
- 6 large eggs
- Salt to taste
- Olive oil for frying

TORTILLA ESPAÑOLA

INSTRUCTIONS

1. Heat a generous amount of olive oil in a non-stick frying pan over medium heat.
2. Add the potatoes and onion, and cook until tender but not browned, stirring occasionally, for about 10-15 minutes.
3. In a large bowl, whisk the eggs and season with salt.
4. Drain the potatoes and onion, then add to the beaten eggs, stirring to combine.
5. Heat a bit more olive oil in the pan, then pour in the egg mixture.
6. Cook over medium-low heat until the edges set. Carefully flip the omelet and cook the other side until golden and cooked through.
7. Slide onto a plate, cut into wedges, and serve warm or at room temperature.

Nutrition

Calories: 350, Protein: 25g,
Carbohydrates: 20g, Fat: 20g

Prep Time:
20 Mins

Cook Time:
30 Mins

Serving: 4

INGREDIENTS

- /2 lb. ground beef
- /2 lb. ground pork
- $1/4$ cup breadcrumbs
- 1 egg
- 2 cloves garlic, minced
- Salt and black pepper to taste
- Olive oil for frying
- For the sauce:
- 1 can (15 oz) crushed tomatoes
- 1/2 onion, finely chopped
- 2 cloves garlic, minced
- Salt and black pepper to taste

ALBÓNDIGAS

INSTRUCTIONS

1. In a bowl, mix together the ground beef, ground pork, breadcrumbs, egg, garlic, salt, and black pepper.
2. Shape into small meatballs, about 1-inch in diameter.
3. Heat olive oil in a skillet over medium-high heat and brown the meatballs on all sides.
4. Remove the meatballs and set aside.
5. In the same skillet, sauté the onion and garlic until translucent.
6. Add the crushed tomatoes, season with salt and black pepper, and bring to a simmer.
7. Return the meatballs to the skillet, cover, and simmer for about 20-25 minutes until the meatballs are cooked through.
8. Serve hot, garnished with fresh parsley if desired.

Nutrition

Calories: 50, Protein: 1g,
Carbohydrates: 5g, Fat: 3g

Prep Time:
05 Mins

Cook Time:
10 Mins

Serving: 4

INGREDIENTS

- 8 oz Padrón peppers
- Olive oil for frying
- Sea salt to taste

PIMIENTOS DE PADRÓN

INSTRUCTIONS

1. Heat a good amount of olive oil in a frying pan over medium-high heat.
2. Add the Padrón peppers and cook, turning occasionally, until blistered and slightly charred.
3. Remove from the heat, drain on paper towels, and sprinkle with sea salt.
4. Serve immediately as a hot tapa.

Nutrition

Calories: 283g, Protein: 11g,
Carbohydrates: 25g, Fat: 16g

**Prep Time:
20 Mins**

**Cook Time:
10 Mins**

Serving: 4

INGREDIENTS

- 2 tablespoons olive oil
- 2 tablespoons unsalted butter
- 1/4 cup all-purpose flour,
  plus more for dredging
- 1 cup milk
- 1/2 cup cooked ham, chicken, or
  cheese, finely chopped
- 1/2 cup mashed potato
- Salt and black pepper to taste
- 1 egg, beaten
- Breadcrumbs for coating
- Vegetable oil for frying

CROQUETAS (CROQUETTES)

INSTRUCTIONS

1. Heat olive oil and butter in a saucepan over medium heat. Stir in the flour and cook for about 2 minutes.
2. Gradually whisk in the milk until smooth, and cook until thickened, about 5 minutes.
3. Mix in mashed potato and chosen filling (ham, chicken or cheese) season with salt and black pepper, and let the mixture cool.
4. Once cooled, shape the mixture into small cylinders, about 2 inches long.
5. Dredge the croquetas in flour, dip in beaten egg, and roll in breadcrumbs.
6. Heat vegetable oil in a deep fryer or large deep skillet over medium-high heat.
7. Fry the croquetas in batches until golden brown and crispy.
8. Drain on paper towels and serve hot.

Nutrition

Calories: 150, Protein: 3g,
Carbohydrates: 25g, Fat: 5g

**Prep Time:
10 Mins**

**Cook Time:
05 Mins**

Serving: 4

INGREDIENTS

- 4 slices rustic bread
- 2 large ripe tomatoes, halved
- 1 clove garlic, halved
- Olive oil for drizzling
- Salt to taste

PAN CON TOMATE

INSTRUCTIONS

1. Grill or toast the bread slices until crispy.
2. Rub the surface of each toast with a cut side of garlic, then with a cut side of tomato, pressing slightly to release the juices.
3. Drizzle each toast with a bit of olive oil and sprinkle with salt.
4. Serve immediately as a simple and flavorful tapa.

Nutrition

Calories: 180, Protein: 25g,
Carbohydrates: 0g, Fat: 8g

Prep Time:
10 Mins

Cook Time:
45 Mins

Serving: 4

INGREDIENTS

- 1 pound octopus, fresh or frozen
- 2 tablespoons olive oil
- 1 teaspoon paprika
- Salt to taste
- 2-3 boiled potatoes, sliced (optional)

PULPO A LA GALLEGA

INSTRUCTIONS

1. If using fresh octopus, freeze it overnight and then thaw to tenderize.
2. Bring a large pot of water to a boil, dip the octopus in the boiling water three times, holding it by the head, then submerge it completely and simmer for about 45 minutes or until tender.
3. Once cooked, let the octopus cool, then slice it into $^1/_2$-inch thick slices.
4. Arrange the octopus slices (and potato slices if using) on a platter, drizzle with olive oil, sprinkle with paprika and salt.
5. Serve warm or at room temperature.

Nutrition

Calories: 250, Protein: 10g,
Carbohydrates: 20g, Fat: 15g

Prep Time: **Cook Time:**
05 Mins **00 Mins**

Serving: 4

INGREDIENTS

- 8 slices of crusty bread
- 8 thin slices of Serrano ham
- Olive oil (optional)

INSTRUCTIONS

1. Arrange slices of bread on the serving platter. Drape a slice of Serrano ham over each slice of bread.
2. Drizzle with a little olive oil if desired. Serve immediately and enjoy.

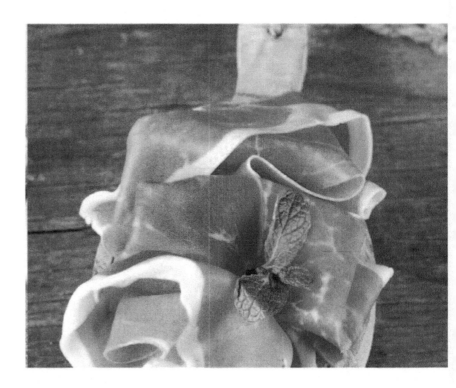

Nutrition

Calories: 350, Protein: 15g,
Carbohydrates: 10g, Fat: 25g

**Prep Time:
05 Mins**

**Cook Time:
20 Mins**

Serving: 4

INGREDIENTS

- 1 pound chorizo sausage, sliced into $1/2$-inch rounds
- 2 cups apple cider

CHORIZO A LA SIDRA

INSTRUCTIONS

1. Place the chorizo slices and cider in a skillet or saucepan. Bring to a simmer over medium heat and cook for about 20 minutes, or until the cider has reduced and the chorizo is cooked through.
2. Serve warm with some of the cider sauce drizzled over.

Nutrition
Calories: 230, Protein: 25g,
Carbohydrates: 6g, Fat: 12g

Prep Time:
10 Mins

Cook Time:
15 Mins

Serving: 4

INGREDIENTS

- 1 pound shrimp, peeled and deveined
- 2 tablespoons olive oil
- 2 cloves garlic, minced
- $1/2$ cup almond meal or finely ground almonds
- 1 cup chicken or vegetable broth
- Salt and black pepper to taste
- Fresh parsley, chopped for garnish

GAMBAS EN SALSA DE ALMENDRAS

INSTRUCTIONS

1. Heat olive oil in a skillet over medium heat.
2. Add the garlic and sauté for about 1 minute until fragrant.
3. Stir in the almond meal and continue cooking for another 2 minutes.
4. Gradually whisk in the broth and bring to a simmer. Cook for about 5-7 minutes until the sauce has thickened slightly.
5. Add the shrimp to the skillet and cook for about 2-3 minutes on each side or until they are pink and opaque.
6. Season with salt and black pepper to taste.
7. Garnish with fresh parsley and serve warm.

Nutrition

Calories: 350, Protein: 3g,
Carbohydrates: 30g, Fat: 25g

**Prep Time:
20 Mins**

**Cook Time:
15 Mins**

Serving: 4

INGREDIENTS

- 2 cups potatoes, diced
- 1 cup carrots, diced
- 1/2 cup peas
- 1/2 cup mayonnaise
- 2 tablespoons olive oil
- Salt and black pepper to taste
- 1/4 cup pickles, diced
- 1/4 cup red peppers, diced

ENSALADILLA RUSA

INSTRUCTIONS

1. Boil the potatoes, carrots, and peas in salted water until tender. Drain and let cool.
2. In a large bowl, mix the mayonnaise and olive oil. Season with salt and black pepper.
3. Add the boiled vegetables, pickles, and red peppers to the mayonnaise mixture and gently stir to combine.
4. Chill the salad in the refrigerator for at least 1 hour before serving.
5. Serve chilled, garnished with extra mayonnaise and some olives if desired.

Nutrition

Calories: 130, Protein: 20g,
Carbohydrates: 1g, Fat: 5g

**Prep Time:
10 Mins**

**Cook Time:
00 Mins**

Serving: 4

INGREDIENTS

- 1 pound fresh anchovies, cleaned
- 1 cup white wine vinegar
- 4 cloves garlic, minced
- 2 tablespoons fresh parsley, finely chopped
- Olive oil for drizzling
- Salt to taste

BOQUERONES EN VINAGRE

INSTRUCTIONS

1. Place the cleaned anchovies in a shallow dish and cover with white wine vinegar. Let marinate in the refrigerator for at least 6 hours, or overnight.
2. Drain the anchovies from the vinegar and arrange on a serving platter.
3. Sprinkle with garlic, parsley, and a little salt.
4. Drizzle with olive oil before serving.

Nutrition

Calories: 250, Protein: 20g,
Carbohydrates: 1g, Fat: 20g

**Prep Time:
10 Mins**

**Cook Time:
10 Mins**

Serving: 4

INGREDIENTS

- 1 pound pork or lamb, cut into 1-inch cubes
- 2 tablespoons olive oil
- 1 teaspoon paprika
- 1 teaspoon ground cumin
- 1/2 teaspoon ground coriander
- Salt and black pepper to taste

PINCHOS MORUNOS

INSTRUCTIONS

1. In a bowl, mix together olive oil, paprika, cumin, coriander, salt, and black pepper.
2. Add the meat and toss to coat. Cover and let marinate in the refrigerator for at least 2 hours, or overnight.
3. Thread the meat onto skewers and grill on medium-high heat for about 10 minutes, turning occasionally, until cooked to your desired level of doneness.
4. Serve hot, garnished with fresh parsley if desired.

Nutrition

Calories: 150, Protein: 1g,
Carbohydrates: 20g, Fat: 10g

Prep Time:
10 Mins

Cook Time:
15 Mins

Serving: 4

INGREDIENTS

- 2 medium eggplants, sliced into 1/2-inch rounds
- Salt
- Olive oil for frying
- Honey for drizzling

BERENJENAS CON MIEL

INSTRUCTIONS

1. Sprinkle the eggplant slices with salt and let sit for about 30 minutes to draw out the moisture.
2. Rinse the eggplant slices and pat dry with paper towels.
3. Heat olive oil in a large frying pan over medium-high heat.
4. Fry the eggplant slices in batches for about 2-3 minutes on each side until golden brown.
5. Drain on paper towels and drizzle with honey before serving.

Nutrition

Calories: 100, Protein: 2g,
Carbohydrates: 15g, Fat: 5g

**Prep Time:
10 Mins**

**Cook Time:
45 Mins**

Serving: 4

INGREDIENTS

- 2 red bell peppers, halved and seeded
- 1 eggplant, sliced into 1/2-inch rounds
- 2 onions, halved
- Olive oil
- Salt and black pepper to taste

ESCALIVADA

INSTRUCTIONS

1. Preheat the oven to 425°F (220°C).
2. Arrange the vegetables on a baking sheet, drizzle with olive oil, and season with salt and black pepper.
3. Roast for about 45 minutes, or until the vegetables are tender and slightly charred.
4. Allow to cool, then peel the skins from the peppers and eggplant. Slice the vegetables into strips and serve at room temperature drizzled with additional olive oil.

Nutrition

Calories: 250, Protein: 4g,
Carbohydrates: 25g, Fat: 15g

Prep Time:
10 Mins

Cook Time:
00 Mins

Serving: 4

INGREDIENTS

- 6 ripe tomatoes, chopped
- 2 cloves garlic
- 2 cups day-old bread, crusts removed and cubed
- 1/4 cup extra virgin olive oil
- Salt to taste
- Hard-boiled eggs and jamón (cured ham) for garnish (optional)

SALMOREJO

INSTRUCTIONS

1. In a blender or food processor, combine the tomatoes, garlic, and bread. Blend until smooth.
2. With the motor running, slowly drizzle in the olive oil until emulsified.
3. Season with salt to taste and chill the soup in the refrigerator for at least 2 hours before serving.
4. Serve chilled, garnished with hard-boiled eggs and jamón if desired.

Nutrition

Calories: 210, Protein: 20g, Carbohydrates: 10g, Fat: 7g

Prep Time: 10 Mins

Cook Time: 20 Mins

Serving: 4

INGREDIENTS

- 2 pounds fresh mussels, cleaned and de-bearded
- 2 tablespoons olive oil
- 1 onion, finely chopped
- 4 cloves garlic, minced
- 1 cup white wine
- 1 cup tomato sauce
- Salt and black pepper to taste
- Fresh parsley for garnish

MEJILLONES A LA MARINERA

INSTRUCTIONS

1. In a large pot, heat the olive oil over medium heat. Add the onion and garlic, and sauté until translucent.
2. Add the white wine and bring to a boil. Add the tomato sauce, salt, and pepper, and stir well.
3. Add the mussels, cover the pot, and cook for about 10 minutes, or until the mussels have opened. Discard any unopened mussels.
4. Garnish with fresh parsley and serve hot.

Nutrition

Calories: 250, Protein: 25g,
Carbohydrates: 0g, Fat: 17g

Prep Time:
10 Mins

Cook Time:
06 Mins

Serving: 4

INGREDIENTS

- 12 fresh sardines, cleaned
- Olive oil for brushing
- Salt
- 2 cloves garlic, minced (optional)

SARDINAS A LA PLANCHA

INSTRUCTIONS

1. Preheat the grill to medium-high heat.
2. Brush the sardines with olive oil and sprinkle with salt. If using garlic, rub it onto the sardines.
3. Grill the sardines for about 3 minutes on each side, or until the skin is crispy and the flesh is flaky.
4. Serve hot, garnished with lemon wedges if desired.

Nutrition

Calories: 280, Protein: 12g,
Carbohydrates: 35g, Fat: 12g

**Prep Time:
10 Mins**

**Cook Time:
20 Mins**

Serving: 4

INGREDIENTS

- 2 tablespoons olive oil
- 4 cloves garlic, minced
- 1 teaspoon paprika
- 1 teaspoon ground cumin
- 2 cans (15 oz each) chickpeas, drained and rinsed
- 10 oz fresh spinach
- Salt and black pepper to taste

ESPINACAS CON GARBANZOS

INSTRUCTIONS

1. In a large frying pan, heat the olive oil over medium heat. Add the garlic, paprika, and cumin, and sauté for about 1 minute.
2. Add the chickpeas and cook for about 10 minutes, stirring occasionally.
3. Add the spinach, cover, and cook for another 5-7 minutes, or until the spinach is wilted.
4. Season with salt and black pepper to taste and serve warm.

Nutrition

Calories: 200, Protein: 20g,
Carbohydrates: 1g, Fat: 13g

Prep Time:
10 Mins

Cook Time:
10 Mins

Serving: 4

INGREDIENTS

- 1 pound dogfish or other firm white fish, cut into bite-sized pieces
- 1/2 cup white wine vinegar
- 2 cloves garlic, minced
- 1 teaspoon paprika
- 1/2 teaspoon ground cumin
- Salt and black pepper to taste
- Olive oil for frying

CAZON EN ADOBO

INSTRUCTIONS

1. In a shallow dish, mix together the vinegar, garlic, paprika, cumin, salt, and black pepper. Add the fish and toss to coat. Cover and let marinate in the refrigerator for at least 2 hours, or overnight.
2. Heat olive oil in a frying pan over medium-high heat. Remove the fish from the marinade and fry for about 3-5 minutes on each side, or until golden and crispy.
3. Drain on paper towels and serve hot.

Nutrition
Calories: 180, Protein: 10g,
Carbohydrates: 10g, Fat: 10g

Prep Time:
15 Mins

Cook Time:
20 Mins

Serving: 4

INGREDIENTS

- 12 piquillo peppers
- 1 cup cooked seafood or ground meat (such as crab, shrimp, or sausage)
- 1/2 cup cream cheese
- Salt and black pepper to taste
- Olive oil for drizzling

PIQUILLOS RELLENOS

INSTRUCTIONS

1. Preheat the oven to 375°F (190°C).
2. In a bowl, mix together the seafood or meat, cream cheese, salt, and black pepper.
3. Stuff each piquillo pepper with the mixture and place in a baking dish.
4. Drizzle with olive oil and bake for about 20 minutes, or until the peppers are heated through and slightly crispy on top. Serve warm.

Nutrition
Calories: 260, Protein: 30g,
Carbohydrates: 8g, Fat: 12g

Prep Time: **Cook Time:**
15 Mins **1 hour**

Serving: 4

INGREDIENTS

- 1 rabbit, cut into pieces
- Salt and black pepper to taste
- 2 tablespoons olive oil
- 1 onion, finely chopped
- 4 cloves garlic, minced
- 1 cup tomato sauce
- 1 cup chicken broth
- 1 teaspoon paprika
- Fresh parsley for garnish

CONEJO EN SALMOREJO

INSTRUCTIONS

1. Season the rabbit pieces with salt and black pepper.
2. In a large pot, heat the olive oil over medium-high heat. Add the rabbit pieces and brown on all sides.
3. Add the onion and garlic, and sauté until translucent.
4. Stir in the tomato sauce, chicken broth, and paprika. Bring to a boil, then reduce heat to low and simmer for about 45 minutes, or until the rabbit is tender.
5. Garnish with fresh parsley and serve hot.

Nutrition

Calories: 170, Protein: 10g,
Carbohydrates: 8g, Fat: 7g

**Prep Time:
10 Mins**

**Cook Time:
20 Mins**

Serving: 4

INGREDIENTS

- 2 pounds clams, cleaned
- 2 tablespoons olive oil
- 4 cloves garlic, minced
- 1/2 cup white wine
- 1/2 cup tomato sauce
- Salt and black pepper to taste
- Fresh parsley for garnish

ALMEJAS A LA MARINERA

INSTRUCTIONS

1. In a large pot, heat the olive oil over medium heat. Add the garlic and sauté for 1-2 minutes.
2. Add the white wine, tomato sauce, salt, and black pepper. Bring to a boil.
3. Add the clams, cover the pot, and simmer for about 10 minutes, or until the clams have opened. Discard any unopened clams.
4. Garnish with fresh parsley and serve hot.

Nutrition

Calories: 150, Protein: 3g,
Carbohydrates: 15g, Fat: 8g

Prep Time:
05 Mins

Cook Time:
05 Mins

Serving: 4

INSTRUCTIONS

1. Toast the bread slices until crispy.
2. Spread a tablespoon of sobrasada on each slice of toast.
3. Drizzle with olive oil and serve warm.

INGREDIENTS

- 4 slices of bread
- 4 tablespoons sobrasada
- Olive oil for drizzling

Nutrition

Calories: 160, Protein: 7g,
Carbohydrates: 8g, Fat: 11g

**Prep Time:
10 Mins**

**Cook Time:
20 Mins**

Serving: 4

INGREDIENTS

- 2 tablespoons olive oil
- 1/2 onion, chopped
- 1/2 bell pepper, chopped
- 2 cloves garlic, minced
- 1 cup tomato sauce
- 4 large eggs
- Salt and black pepper to taste
- 1/4 cup cooked chorizo or ham, diced (optional)

HUEVOS A LA FLAMENCA

INSTRUCTIONS

1. Preheat the oven to 400°F (200°C).
2. In a frying pan, heat the olive oil over medium heat. Add the onion, bell pepper, and garlic, and sauté until tender.
3. Stir in the tomato sauce and simmer for about 5 minutes. If using, add the chorizo or ham.
4. Divide the sauce among 4 oven-proof dishes. Crack an egg into each dish and season with salt and black pepper.
5. Bake for about 10-12 minutes, or until the eggs are cooked to your desired consistency.
6. Serve hot.

Nutrition

Calories: 190, Protein: 25g,
Carbohydrates: 8g, Fat: 7g

Prep Time:
10 Mins

Cook Time:
30 Mins

Serving: 4

INGREDIENTS

- 1 lb. salted cod, soaked overnight and drained
- 2 tablespoons olive oil
- 1 onion, finely chopped
- 4 cloves garlic, minced
- 1 cup tomato sauce
- 1/2 cup red bell pepper, roasted and peeled
- Salt and black pepper to taste

BACALAO A LA VIZCAíNA

INSTRUCTIONS

1. In a large frying pan, heat the olive oil over medium heat. Add the onion and garlic, and sauté until translucent.
2. Stir in the tomato sauce and red bell pepper, and simmer for about 10 minutes.
3. Add the cod to the sauce and cook for another 10-15 minutes, or until the fish is cooked through.
4. Season with salt and black pepper to taste and serve hot.

Nutrition

Calories: 220, Protein: 20g,
Carbohydrates: 6g, Fat: 12g

Prep Time:
20 Mins

Cook Time:
10 Mins

Serving: 4

INGREDIENTS

- 1/2 lb mussels, cleaned
- 1/2 lb squid, cleaned and
  sliced into rings
- 1/2 cup red bell pepper, diced
- 1/2 cup green bell pepper, diced
- 1/4 cup red onion, finely chopped
- 2 tablespoons fresh parsley,
  chopped
- 1/4 cup olive oil
- 1/2 lb shrimp, peeled
  and deveined
- 2 tablespoons red wine vinegar
- Salt and black pepper to taste

SALPICÓN DE MARISCO

INSTRUCTIONS

1. In a pot of boiling water, cook the shrimp, mussels, and
   squid separately until they are cooked through. Drain and let
   them cool.
2. In a large bowl, mix together the cooked seafood,
   bell peppers, red onion, and parsley.
3. In a small bowl, whisk together the olive oil, red wine
   vinegar, salt, and black pepper. Pour the vinaigrette over
   the seafood mixture and toss to coat.
4. Chill the salad for at least 1 hour before serving to allow
   the flavors to meld.

Nutrition

Calories: 100, Protein: 3g,
Carbohydrates: 4g, Fat: 8g

Prep Time:
05 Mins

Cook Time:
10 Mins

Serving: 4

INGREDIENTS

- 2 tablespoons olive oil
- 4 cloves garlic, minced
- 16 oz mushrooms, sliced
- 2 tablespoons fresh parsley, chopped
- Salt and black pepper to taste

CHAMPIÑONES AL AJILLO

INSTRUCTIONS

1. Heat the olive oil in a frying pan over medium heat. Add the garlic and sauté for 1 minute.
2. Add the mushrooms and cook for about 10 minutes, or until they are golden and tender.
3. Stir in the parsley, salt, and black pepper, and serve hot.

Nutrition

Calories: 320, Protein: 20g,
Carbohydrates: 4g, Fat: 24g

Prep Time:
10 Mins

Cook Time:
30 Mins

Serving: 4

INGREDIENTS

- 4 chicken thighs, bone-in, skin-on
- Salt and black pepper to taste
- 2 tablespoons olive oil
- 10 cloves garlic, minced
- 1/2 cup white wine
- 1/2 cup chicken broth
- 2 tablespoons fresh parsley, chopped

POLLO AL AJILLO

INSTRUCTIONS

1. Season the chicken thighs with salt and black pepper.
2. In a large skillet, heat the olive oil over medium-high heat. Add the chicken thighs, skin-side down, and cook for about 5 minutes on each side, or until they are golden brown.
3. Reduce the heat to medium, add the garlic, and sauté for 1 minute.
4. Pour in the white wine and chicken broth, and simmer for about 20 minutes, or until the chicken is cooked through.
5. Garnish with fresh parsley and serve hot.

Nutrition

Calories: 300, Protein: 15g,
Carbohydrates: 25g, Fat: 15g

Prep Time:
20 Mins

Cook Time:
25 Mins

Serving: 4

INGREDIENTS

- 1/2 lb canned tuna, drained
- 1/4 cup onion, finely chopped
- 1/4 cup bell pepper, finely chopped
- 2 tablespoons tomato sauce
- Salt and black pepper to taste
- 1 sheet of puff pastry (homemade or store-bought)
- 1 egg, beaten (for egg wash)

INSTRUCTIONS

1. In a bowl, mix together the tuna, onion, bell pepper, tomato sauce, salt, and black pepper.
2. Roll out the puff pastry on a floured surface and cut it in half.
3. Place half of the tuna mixture on one half of the pastry, leaving a small border around the edges. Fold the pastry over the filling and crimp the edges to seal.
4. Repeat with the other half of the pastry and filling.
5. Place the empanadas on a baking sheet, brush them with the beaten egg, and bake in a preheated 375°F (190°C) oven for about 25 minutes, or until they are golden brown and crispy.

Nutrition

Calories: 210, Protein: 25g,
Carbohydrates: 6g, Fat: 10g

**Prep Time:
10 Mins**

**Cook Time:
10 Mins**

Serving: 4

INGREDIENTS

- 1 lb shrimp, peeled and deveined (if desried)
- 2 tablespoons olive oil
- 2 cloves garlic, minced
- 1/4 cup breadcrumbs
- 1/4 cup Parmesan cheese, grated
- Salt and black pepper to taste
- Fresh parsley for garnish

GAMBAS AL HORNO

INSTRUCTIONS

1. Preheat the oven to 400°F (200°C).
2. In a bowl, toss the shrimp with the olive oil, garlic, breadcrumbs, Parmesan cheese, salt, and black pepper.
3. Spread the shrimp out on a baking sheet and bake for about 10 minutes, or until they are pink and opaque.
4. Garnish with fresh parsley and serve hot.

Nutrition

Calories: 90, Protein: 12g,
Carbohydrates: 1g, Fat: 4g

Prep Time:
15 Mins

Cook Time:
4-6 hour

Serving: 4

INGREDIENTS

- 1/2 lb fresh anchovies, cleaned and filleted
- 1 cup white wine vinegar
- 2 cloves garlic, minced
- 2 tablespoons fresh parsley, finely chopped
- Olive oil for drizzling
- Salt to taste

ANCHOAS EN VINAGRE

INSTRUCTIONS

1. Place the anchovy fillets in a shallow dish and cover with white wine vinegar. Cover and refrigerate for 4-6 hours to marinate.
2. Drain the anchovies and pat them dry with paper towels. Arrange them on a serving platter.
3. Sprinkle with garlic, parsley, and a drizzle of olive oil. Season with salt to taste and serve.

Nutrition

Calories: 110, Protein: 14g,
Carbohydrates: 2g, Fat: 5g

**Prep Time:
10 Mins**

**Cook Time:
06 Mins**

Serving: 4

INGREDIENTS

- 12 large scallops
- 2 tablespoons olive oil
- Salt and black pepper to taste
- Lemon wedges for serving

ZAMBURIÑAS A LA PLANCHA

INSTRUCTIONS

1. Preheat a grill or grill pan to medium-high heat.
2. Brush the scallops with olive oil on both sides and season with salt and black pepper.
3. Grill the scallops for about 3 minutes on each side, or until they are opaque and have grill marks.
4. Serve hot with lemon wedges.

Nutrition
Calories: 260, Protein: 10g,
Carbohydrates: 15g, Fat: 18g

Prep Time:
10 Mins

Cook Time:
25 Mins

Serving: 4

INGREDIENTS

- 4 tablespoons olive oil
- 8 cloves garlic, minced
- 4 slices day-old bread
- 1 teaspoon paprika
- 4 cups chicken or vegetable broth
- 4 eggs
- Salt to taste

SOPA DE AJO

INSTRUCTIONS

1. Heat the olive oil in a large pot over medium heat. Add the garlic and sauté until golden brown.
2. Add the bread slices and cook until they are toasted, flipping once.
3. Stir in the paprika and add the broth. Bring to a simmer and cook for about 15 minutes.
4. Carefully crack the eggs into the soup, keeping them separate. Cover and simmer for about 5 minutes, or until the eggs are poached to your liking.
5. Season with salt to taste and serve hot.

Nutrition

Calories: 250, Protein: 22g,
Carbohydrates: 2g, Fat: 12g

Prep Time:
10 Mins

Cook Time:
20 Mins

Serving: 4

INGREDIENTS

- 4 pork tenderloin medallions
- Salt and black pepper to taste
- 2 tablespoons olive oil
- 1/2 cup whiskey
- 1/2 cup chicken or vegetable broth
- 2 cloves garlic, minced

SOLOMILLO AL WHISKY

INSTRUCTIONS

1. Season the pork medallions with salt and black pepper on both sides.
2. Heat the olive oil in a skillet over medium-high heat. Add the pork medallions and sear for about 4 minutes on each side, or until they are golden brown and cooked to your desired doneness.
3. Remove the pork from the skillet and set aside. Add the whiskey, broth, and garlic to the skillet and bring to a simmer. Cook for about 5 minutes, or until the sauce has reduced by half.
4. Return the pork to the skillet and cook for an additional 2 minutes, or until heated through. Serve hot with whiskey sauce.

Nutrition

Calories: 350, Protein: 20g,
Carbohydrates: 20g, Fat: 20g

Prep Time:
20 Mins

Cook Time:
30 Mins

Serving: 4

INGREDIENTS

- 4 bell peppers, halved and seeds removed
- 1/2 lb ground beef
- 1/2 lb ground pork
- 1/4 cup onion, finely chopped
- 2 cloves garlic, minced
- 1/2 cup cooked rice
- 1 cup tomato sauce
- Salt and black pepper to taste
- Olive oil for drizzling

PIMIENTOS RELLENOS DE CARNE

INSTRUCTIONS

1. Preheat the oven to 375°F (190°C).
2. In a large bowl, mix together the ground beef, ground pork, onion, garlic, rice, half of the tomato sauce, salt, and black pepper.
3. Stuff each bell pepper half with the meat mixture and place them in a baking dish.
4. Spoon the remaining tomato sauce over the stuffed peppers and drizzle with olive oil.
5. Cover with aluminum foil and bake for about 30 minutes, or until the peppers are tender and the meat is cooked through. Serve hot.

Nutrition

Calories: 350, Protein: 14g,
Carbohydrates: 10g, Fat: 28g

**Prep Time:
05 Mins**

**Cook Time:
10 Mins**

Serving: 4

INGREDIENTS

- 1 lb Morcilla de Burgos (Spanish blood sausage)
- Olive oil for frying

MORCILLA DE BURGOS

INSTRUCTIONS

1. Slice the morcilla into 1/2-inch thick rounds.
2. Heat a bit of olive oil in a frying pan over medium heat. Add the morcilla slices and fry for about 4-5 minutes on each side until crispy and heated through.
3. Serve hot as a tapa.

Nutrition

Calories: 200, Protein: 10g,
Carbohydrates: 20g, Fat: 10g

**Prep Time:
05 Mins**

**Cook Time:
00 Mins**

Serving: 4

INGREDIENTS

- 8 ounces Manchego cheese, sliced
- 4 ounces membrillo (quince paste), sliced

QUESO MANCHEGO CON MEMBRILLO

INSTRUCTIONS

1. Arrange slices of Manchego cheese and membrillo on a serving platter.
2. Serve as a tapa, allowing guests to pair a slice of cheese with a slice of membrillo.

Nutrition

Calories: 120, Protein: 2g,
Carbohydrates: 4g, Fat: 11g

**Prep Time:
10 Mins**

**Cook Time:
05 Mins**

Serving: 4

INGREDIENTS

- 1 lb asparagus spears, trimmed
- 1/4 cup olive oil
- 2 tablespoons red wine vinegar
- 1 teaspoon Dijon mustard
- Salt and black pepper to taste

ESPÁRRAGOS A LA VINAGRETA

INSTRUCTIONS

1. Steam or boil the asparagus for about 4-5 minutes, or until tender-crisp. Drain and set aside to cool.
2. In a small bowl, whisk together the olive oil, red wine vinegar, Dijon mustard, salt, and black pepper.
3. Arrange the asparagus on a serving platter and drizzle with the vinaigrette. Serve chilled or at room temperature.

Nutrition

Calories: 110, Protein: 2g,
Carbohydrates: 2g, Fat: 10g

Prep Time:
10 Mins

Cook Time:
00 Mins

Serving: 4

INGREDIENTS

- 4 heads Little Gem lettuce, halved
- 1/4 cup Roquefort cheese, crumbled
- 2 tablespoons olive oil
- 1 tablespoon red wine vinegar
- Salt and black pepper to taste

COgOLLOS AL ROQUEFORT

INSTRUCTIONS

1. Arrange the lettuce halves on a serving platter.
2. In a small bowl, whisk together the olive oil, red wine vinegar, salt, and black pepper. Drizzle over the lettuce.
3. Sprinkle the Roquefort cheese over the lettuce and serve.

Nutrition

Calories: 280, Protein: 8g,
Carbohydrates: 24g, Fat: 18g

Prep Time:
15 Mins

Cook Time:
30 mins

Serving: 8

INGREDIENTS

- 2 cups almond flour
- 1 cup sugar
- 4 large eggs
- Zest of 1 lemon
- 1/4 teaspoon almond extract
- Powdered sugar for dusting
- Cross of Saint James stencil (optional)

TARTA DE SANTIAGO

INSTRUCTIONS

1. Preheat the oven to 350°F (175°C). Grease a 9-inch round cake pan and line with parchment paper.
2. In a large bowl, mix together the almond flour and sugar. Beat in the eggs, one at a time, until well combined.
3. Stir in the lemon zest and almond extract.
4. Pour the batter into the prepared cake pan and spread evenly.
5. Bake for about 30 minutes, or until the cake is golden brown and a toothpick inserted into the center comes out clean.
6. Allow the cake to cool in the pan for about 10 minutes, then transfer to a wire rack to cool completely.
7. Before serving, place the Cross of Saint James stencil (if using) on top of the cake and dust with powdered sugar.

Nutrition

Calories: 180, Protein: 0g,
Carbohydrates: 4g, Fat: 18g

Prep Time:
10 Mins

Cook Time:
2 hour

Serving: 4

MARINATED OLIVES

INSTRUCTIONS

1. In a large bowl, combine all the ingredients and toss well to coat the olives evenly.
2. Cover and refrigerate for at least 2 hours, or overnight for better flavor infusion.
3. Serve chilled or at room temperature.

INGREDIENTS

- 2 cups mixed olives (green, black, Kalamata, etc.)
- 1/4 cup extra virgin olive oil
- Zest of 1 lemon
- 2 cloves garlic, minced
- 1 teaspoon red pepper flakes
- 2 teaspoons fresh thyme leaves

Nutrition
Calories: 240, Protein: 40g,
Carbohydrates: 6g, Fat: 6g

Prep Time:
10 Mins

Cook Time:
20 Mins

Serving: 4

INGREDIENTS

- 4 tuna steaks
- 2 tablespoons olive oil
- 1 large onion, thinly sliced
- 3 cloves garlic, minced
- 1/2 cup tomato sauce
- Salt and pepper to taste

ATÚN ENCEBOLLADO

INSTRUCTIONS

1. Heat olive oil in a skillet over medium-high heat. Season tuna steaks with salt and pepper.
2. Sear the tuna steaks for about 2 minutes on each side, then remove from the skillet and set aside.
3. In the same skillet, sauté the onion and garlic until soft and translucent.
4. Stir in the tomato sauce and bring to a simmer.
5. Return the tuna steaks to the skillet, cover, and simmer for about 10-15 minutes, or until the tuna is cooked to your desired doneness.
6. Serve hot with the onion and tomato sauce spooned over the top.

Nutrition

Calories: 250, Protein: 10g,
Carbohydrates: 20g, Fat: 15g

**Prep Time:
15 Mins**

**Cook Time:
00 Mins**

Serving: 4

INGREDIENTS

- 8 small Spanish rolls (barras or molletes), halved
- Assorted fillings:
- Jamón Serrano or Ibérico
- Manchego cheese
- Spanish chorizo
- Tuna (atún)
- Roasted red peppers (pimientos)
- Lettuce
- Tomato
- Extra virgin olive oil
- Salt and pepper to taste

MONTADITOS

INSTRUCTIONS

1. Prepare the assorted fillings. Slice the ham, chorizo, and cheese thinly, and slice or shred the other ingredients as necessary.
2. Drizzle a little extra virgin olive oil on the cut side of each roll, then season lightly with salt and pepper.
3. Assemble the montanites by placing your choice of fillings between the halves of each roll. You can create a variety of flavor combinations by mixing and matching the fillings.
4. Serve immediately or wrap in foil and warm in a 350°F (175°C) oven for about 5-10 minutes before serving.

Nutrition

Calories: 70, Protein: 5g,
Carbohydrates: 8g, Fat: 2g

**Prep Time:
10 Mins**

**Cook Time:
00 Mins**

Serving: 4

INGREDIENTS

- 1 ripe melon, cut into thin wedges
- 8 thin slices of jamón serrano or prosciutto

MELÓN CON JAMÓN

INSTRUCTIONS

1. Wrap each slice of ham around a wedge of melon.
2. Arrange on a serving platter and serve chilled or at room temperature.

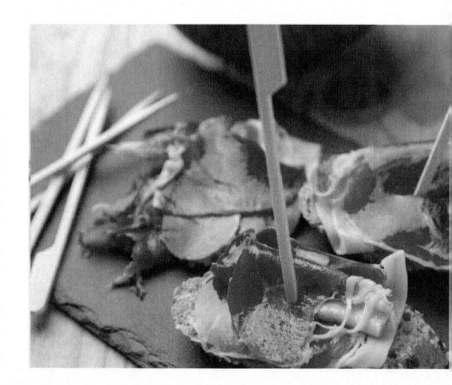

Nutrition

Calories: 350, Protein: 18g,
Carbohydrates: 40g, Fat: 12g

**Prep Time:
15 Mins**

**Cook Time:
10 Mins**

Serving: 4

INGREDIENTS

- 2 cups calamari rings
- 1/2 cup flour
- Salt and pepper to taste
- Vegetable oil for frying
- 4 small baguettes, halved
- Mayonnaise and/or aioli, optional

BOCADILLO DE CALAMARES

INSTRUCTIONS

1. Season the calamari rings with salt and pepper, then toss with flour to coat.
2. Heat vegetable oil in a deep fryer or large pot to 350°F (175°C).
3. Fry the calamari rings in batches for about 2-3 minutes, or until golden brown and crispy.
4. Drain on paper towels.
5. Fill each baguette with a generous amount of fried calamari.
6. Serve hot, with mayonnaise and/or aioli if desired.

Nutrition

Calories: 210 kcal, Protein: 30g,
Carbohydrates: 5g, Fat: 7g

**Prep Time:
15 Mins**

**Cook Time:
1 hour 30 mins**

Serving: 4

INGREDIENTS

- 4 boneless, skinless chicken breasts
- 3 tablespoons achiote paste
- 1/2 cup orange juice
- 1/4 cup lime juice
- 4 cloves garlic, minced
- 1 teaspoon cumin
- 1 teaspoon oregano
- Salt and pepper to taste
- 2 banana leaves (optional)

POLLO A LA PIBIL

INSTRUCTIONS

1. In a bowl, mix together the achiote paste, orange juice, lime juice, garlic, cumin, oregano, salt, and pepper to create the marinade.

2. Place the chicken breasts in a shallow dish and pour the marinade over them. Cover and refrigerate for at least 4 hours, or overnight for best flavor.

3. If using banana leaves, lay them in a baking dish, placing the chicken on top. If not, simply place the chicken in a greased baking dish.

4. Cover the dish with foil and bake in a preheated oven at 325°F (160°C) for about 1 hour and 30 minutes, or until the chicken is tender and cooked through.

5. (Optional) For a more traditional street food style, after baking, you could shred the chicken and serve it on tortillas with your choice of toppings like fresh cilantro, chopped onions, and a squeeze of lime.

Nutrition

Calories: 220 kcal, Protein: 10g,
Carbohydrates: 20g, Fat: 11g

**Prep Time:
10 Mins**

**Cook Time:
5-10 Mins**

Serving: 4

INGREDIENTS

- 8 slices of baguette or rustic bread
- 200g goat cheese, sliced
  or crumbled
- 2 tablespoons honey or maple
  syrup (optional)
- 2 tablespoons walnuts, chopped
  (optional)
- Fresh thyme or rosemary for
  garnish (optional)

TOSTAS DE QUESO DE

CABRA

INSTRUCTIONS

1. Preheat the oven to 375°F (190°C).
2. Arrange the bread slices on a baking sheet and toast in the oven for about 5 minutes until they are crisp.
3. Top each toast with slices or crumbles of goat cheese.
4. Return the toast to the oven and bake for another 5-10 minutes until the cheese is slightly melted and bubbly.
5. (Optional) Drizzle with honey or maple syrup, sprinkle with chopped walnuts, and garnish with fresh thyme or rosemary before serving.

Nutrition

Calories: 280 kcal, Protein: 11g,
Carbohydrates: 20g, Fat: 18g

**Prep Time:
05 Mins**

**Cook Time:
10 Mins**

Serving: 4

INGREDIENTS

- 4 slices of hearty bread
- 100g cheese (Manchego, Cheddar, or your choice), sliced
- 2 tablespoons butter
- Olive oil for brushing

QUESO A LA PLANCHA

INSTRUCTIONS

1. Preheat a grill or stovetop griddle over medium heat.
2. Butter one side of each slice of bread.
3. Place the cheese slices on the unbuttered side of 2 slices of bread, then top with the remaining slices, buttered side facing out.
4. Lightly brush the grill or griddle with olive oil.
5. Place the sandwiches on the grill or griddle and cook for about 4-5 minutes on each side, until the bread is toasted, and the cheese is melted.

Conclusion

As we close the final pages of "Tapas Tradition," it is our hope that you have not only discovered the diversity and vibrancy of Spanish tapas but also felt the joy and camaraderie that comes with sharing these small plates. The journey through these recipes is more than a culinary venture; it's an embrace of a lifestyle that celebrates the small moments and the big flavors.

Through the 50 recipes we've explored together, you've been equipped with the tools to recreate the spirit of a Spanish tapas bar in your own home. Each dish you've prepared is a thread in the larger tapestry of Spanish culture, a story told on a plate, meant to be passed around and enjoyed amongst friends and family.

As you continue to cook these tapas, remember that each ingredient you chop, each pot you stir, and every plate you serve continues the tradition of sharing and enjoyment that is at the heart of Spanish cuisine. May the laughter and warmth that accompany tapas dining fill your home with happiness and your life with good company.

Whether you've cooked for a crowd or savored these bites in quiet solitude, we trust that the flavors have transported you to the sun-drenched terraces of Spain. Until we meet again, keep the tapas tradition alive and continue to share the love and flavor of Spain's rich culinary heritage. ¡Hasta la próxima!

Printed in Great Britain
by Amazon

42129244R00059